THE SON OF A DUCK IS A FLOATER

Primrose Arnander **Ashkhain Skipwith**

with illustrations by
Kathryn Lamb

STACEY INTERNATIONAL
LONDON

The Son of a Duck is a Floater
Published by Stacey International
128 Kensington Church Street
London W8 4BH
Telex 298768 Stacey G

ISBN 0 905743 41 5

Set in Monophoto Plantin by
SX Composing Ltd, Essex, England
Set in Monophoto Naskh by
Aurora Press Ltd, London
Printed and Bound by
Butler & Tanner Ltd, Somerset, England

Note on transliteration

The form of transliteration used is one that has been developed over recent years, somewhat simplified in the hope that it will help those with little or no Arabic to articulate the proverbs in their original language. Most of the transliterations are self-evident, but a few comments may be useful.

ẓ ṭ ḍ ṣ ḥ	*are hard letters, heavily pronounced*
dh th	*equivalent to th (as in there and think, respectively)*
ā ū ī	*are long (as in baa, moon, seen)*
kh	*equivalent to ch, as in loch*
gh	*rolled, as the French letter r*
g	*represents the Arabic qaaf (hard q)*
'	*before and after letters, represents the Arabic letters ayn and hamza, which have no English equivalent. The exact sound cannot be explained easily in writing, the nearest equivalent being a glottal stop or hesitation.*

Authors' Preface

We have assembled this small collection of Arab proverbs and sayings in the hope of giving some entertainment to our Arab and non-Arab readers. We do not set ourselves up as researchers or scholars, but have collected the proverbs, all of which are in common use, from friends and acquaintances. The proverbs are not all from one country or one dialect of Arabic, but are generally known in the Eastern part of the Arab world.

Below each Arabic proverb we print as exact a transliteration as possible, to assist readers who do not know the language. We also provide a handwritten English translation which is faithful to the Arabic and, in most cases, a similar English proverb (printed in italics) or interesting comparison (with the prefix 'cf.'. In the absence of any parallel, a short explanation of the proverb is given where appropriate.

We count ourselves especially fortunate in our artistic collaborator, Kathryn Lamb, who has lived for some years in the Arab world, and is now making a name for herself as a cartoonist in England.

We also take this opportunity to thank all those who have helped us in one way or another in the production of this book, and in particular Mr. Hatem El-Khalidi, who has given unstintingly of his advice and support, and who has written an introduction for us.

Primrose Arnander

Ashkhain Skipwith

Introduction

"To understand a people, acquaint yourself with their proverbs". Thus goes an old Arab saying.

This little book of Arab proverbs attempts to open the door for such an understanding. It also shows that many, indeed the majority, of proverbs quoted are identical in thought, if not in word, to the proverbs of the West, thus belying the poet's words "Oh, East is East, and West is West, and never the twain shall meet."

Let us hope that this book will contribute to a real meeting of the East and West, for in that will lie the true salvation of mankind.

Hatem El-Khalidi
Jeddah

من جد وجد ومن زرع حصد

Man jadda wajad wa man zara'a ḥaṣad.

He who perseveres finds and he who sows harvests

الإيمان يزحزح الجبال

Al īmān yuzaḥziḥ al jibāl.

Faith moves mountains

A proverb shared by both languages.

إن الطيور على أشكالها تقع

Innaṭṭuyūra 'alā ashkāliha taqa'.

Birds alight among their like

Birds of a feather flock together

عمل من الحبة قبة

'Amal min al ḩabbah gubba.

He made a dome from a seed

cf. *to make a mountain out of a molehill*

أدعي على ولدي وأكره من يقول آمين

Ad' ī 'ala waladī wa akrahu man yugūl āmīn.

I curse my son and hate the one who says Amen

Family solidarity!

كب القهوة خير

Kab al gahwa khayr.

Spilling coffee is a good omen

Bad luck often brings good luck in its wake.

إذا كان حبيبك من عسل لا تلحسه كله

Idha kan ḫabībak min 'asal lā talḫasu kullu.

If your loved one is made of honey don't lick him all up

من راقب الناس مات همّا

Man rāgab an nās māta hamman.

He who watches others obsessively dies of chagrin

cf. *He that gazes upon the sun shall at last be blind*

سلاح المرأة دموعها

Silāḥ al mar'a dumū'ahā.

The weapon of a woman is her tears

cf. *Trust not a woman when she weeps*

من اتّكل على رغيف أخيه مات جوعًا

Man ittakala 'alā raghīfi akhīhi māta jū'an.

He who relies on his brother's loaf dies of hunger

He who depends on another dines ill and sups worse

إسأل مجرّب ولا تسأل طبيب

Is'al mujarrib wala tas'al ṭabīb.

Ask one who has experience rather than a physician

Experience without learning is better than learning without experience

عرج الجمل من شفّته

'Araj al jamal min shiffatu.

The camel limped from its split lip

cf. *A bad workman blames his tools*

الجار قبل الدار

Al jār gabl ad-dār.

Choose the neighbour before the house

We can live without friends, but not without neighbours

SOLD

اللى يكبر حجره لا يضرب

Illi yikabbir ḥajaru lā yaḍrib.

He who chooses too large a stone cannot strike with it

Don't bite off more than you can chew

لكل جوادٍ كَبْوة ولكل عالم هفوة

Li kulli jawad kabwa wa likulli 'ālim hafwa.

To every horse a stumble and to every sage a lapse

cf. *Homer sometimes nods,* and *'Tis a good horse that never stumbles*

عنزة ولو طارت

'anza wa law ṭārat.

Still a goat, even if she flies!

What obstinacy!

أنا وأخي على ابن عمي   وأنا وابن عمي على الغريب

Anā wa akhī 'ala ibn 'ammī wa anā wa ibn 'ammī 'ala-l-gharīb.

My brother and I against my cousin,
My cousin and I against a stranger

cf. *Blood is thicker than water*

حظه بيفلق الحجر

Ḥaẓu biyiflig al ḥajar.

His luck splits the stone

He has the devil's own luck

المرء بآدابه لا بثيابه

Almar'u bi ādābihi lā bi thiyābihi.

A man is known by his manners, not by his clothes

Fine feathers do not make fine birds

اللي فات مات

Illi fāt māt.

What is past is dead

Let bygones be bygones

رُبَّ صدفة خيرٌ من ميعاد

Rubba ṣudfa khayrun min mī'ād.

A chance encounter may be better than an appointment

عاشرنا واخبرنا

'Āshirnā wa akhbirnā.

Live with us and then judge us

A proverb shared by both languages.

لا يضر السحاب نبح الكلاب

Lā yaḍur as-siḥāb nabḥ al kilāb.

The clouds are not hurt by the baying of dogs

The dog barks in vain at the moon

منها زيارة ومنها تجارة

Minha ziyāra wa minha tijāra.

It is both a social and a business call

cf. *to combine business with pleasure*

إذا رأيتَ نيوبَ الليثِ بارزةً   فلا تظنن أن الليثَ يبتسم

Idhā ra'ayta nuyūb al laythi bārizatan falā taẓunnana ann allaytha yabtasimu.

If the lion bares his teeth, don't assume he is smiling

Things are not always what they seem

وجها يحمّض اللبن

Wijha biyiḥammiḍ al laban.

Her face sours the milk

من تحت الدلف لتحت المزراب

Min taḥt al dalf lataḥt al mizrāb.

From under the drip to under the spout

Out of the frying pan into the fire

يا رايح كثّر ملايح

Ya rāyiḥ kaththir malāyiḥ.

O departing one, leave behind good deeds!

A good deed is never lost

مثل اللى يبيع سمك فى البحر

Mithl ilh yibī' samak fi al baḥar.

It's like selling fish still in the sea

Don't count your chickens before they are hatched

حبل الكذب قصير

Ḥabl al kidhb gaṣīr.

The rope of a lie is short

The liar is sooner caught than the cripple

زى الأطرش فى الزفة

Zay al aṭrash fizzaffa.

He is like a deaf person at a wedding procession

Loud music accompanies the Arab bridegroom to his bride's house. A deaf man would feel totally excluded: *a fish out of water.*

ايش علم الحمير بأكل الزنجبيل

Aysh 'allam al ḥamīr bi akl il Zanjabīl.

What taught the donkeys to eat ginger?

cf. *to cast pearls before swine*

المال يجلب الجنّي مقيدًا

Almālu yajlib al jinnī mugayyadan.

Money delivers the genie bound

He who pays the piper calls the tune

كلام الليل يمحوه النهار

Kalām al layl yamhūhu an-nahār.

The day obliterates the promises of the night

cf. *Vows made in storms are forgotten in calms*

يسرق الكحل من العين

Yasrig al kuḥul min al 'ayn.

He steals the kohl* from the eye

cf. *He'd steal the shirt off your back*

*black eye make-up

اللي مايعرف الصقر يشويه

Illi ma yi'raf iṣ-ṣagr yishwīh.

He who does not recognise the falcon grills it

Regrettable deeds are performed through ignorance.

لا دخان بدون نار

Lā dukhkhān bidūn nār.

No smoke without fire

A proverb shared by both languages.

اللي يجاور الحداد ينكوي بناره

Illi yijāwir al ḥaddad yinkiwī bi nāru.

He who lives beside the blacksmith is branded by his fire

He that touches pitch shall be defiled

ما إن ندمت على سكوتي مرةً   فلقد ندمت على كلامي مرارًا

Mā in nadimtu 'alā sukūtī marratan falagad nadimtu 'alā kalāmī mirāran.

If I have regretted my silence once, I have regretted my chatter many a time

More have repented speech than silence

من علمني حرفاً أصبحت له عبداً

Man 'allamani ḥarfan aṣbaḥtu lahu 'abdan.

I become the slave of he who teaches me one letter

A sign of the high esteem in which education is held.

لا تترك عمل اليوم إلى الغد

Lā tatruk 'amal al yawmi ila al ghadi.

Don't leave today's work until tomorrow

Never put off till tomorrow what can be done today

اللى يسرق البيضة يسرق الجمل

Illi yisrig al bayḍa yisrig al jamal.

He who steals the egg steals the camel

He that will steal an egg will steal an ox

العجلة من الشيطان والتأني من الرحمن

Al 'ajala min ash-shayṭān watta'anni min ar-raḥmān.

Haste is the devil's work and Patience is from the Merciful

Patience is a virtue

*The Merciful is one of the names of God.

الجائع يحلم بسوق العيش

Al ja'i' yiḥlam bi sūg al 'aysh.

The hungry man dreams of the bread market

A hungry man smells meat afar off

ذكرنا القط جانا ينط

Dhakarna al guṭ jānā yinuṭ.

We mentioned the cat, it came bounding

Talk of the devil . . .

ابن البط عوّام

Ibn al baṭ 'awwām.

The son of a duck is a floater

Like father, like son

يد واحدة لا تصفق

Yad wāḥida lā tiṣaffig.

One hand cannot clap

cf. *It takes two to tango*

تقول للقمر غيب وأنا بدالك نقيب

Tigūl lil gamar ghīb wana badālak nagib.

She says to the moon 'Disappear, and I shall take your place'

cf. *Please make no mistake, We are not shy, We really know our worth, the moon and I*
Yum Yum in *The Mikado* (W. S. Gilbert)

قديمك نديمك ولو الجديد أغناك

Gadīmak nadīmak wa law al jadīd aghnāk.

Stay with your old crony even if the new friend enriches you

cf. *Old friends are best*

خالف تعرف

Khālif tu'raf.

Be contrary and be known

مربط عنزة فى دارك ولا فى قصر جارك

Marbaṭ 'anza fī dārāk wala fi gaṣir jārak.

The goat's stall in your own house
is better than your neighbour's palace

There's no place like home

الجمل ما يشوف سنامه

Al jamal mā yishūf sanāmu.

The camel cannot see its own hump

cf. *The pot calls the kettle black*

الأقربون أولى بالمعروف

Al agrabūn awlā bilma 'rūf.

Your relatives have first claim on your favours

Charity begins at home

خير البر عاجله

Khayr al barri 'ā jiluhu.

The best deeds are those done promptly

He gives twice who gives quickly

عند البطون طارت العقول

'ind al buṭūn ṭārat al 'uqūl.

When stomachs are busy minds are lost

cf. *Fat paunches have lean pates*

إذا كثر الربابنة غرقت السفينة

Idha kathira ar-rabābina gharigat as-safīna.

Too many captains sink the ship

Too many cooks spoil the broth

DATES

البعرة تدل البعير

Al ba'ra tadul 'ala al ba'īr.

The camel's dung points to the camel

علمناهم عالشحذة سبقونا عالابواب

'Alamnāhum 'alshiḥda sabagūna 'alabwāb.

We taught them how to beg, they raced us to the gates

cf. *to beat someone at his own game*

ذنب الكلب أعوج ولو حطيت فى خمسين قالب

Dhanab al kalb a 'waj walaw ḥaṭṭaytu fī khamsīn gālib.

The dog's tail remains crooked, even if it is put in fifty moulds

A leopard cannot change its spots

النظافة من الإيمان

Annaẓāfa min al īmān.

Cleanliness is akin to faith

Cleanliness is next to Godliness

مثل الحمام المقطوعة ميته

Mithl al ḥammām al magṭu'a mayyatu.

It's like a public bath with its water cut off

Total chaos; bedlam!

إللى خلّف ما مات

Illi kallaf mā māt.

He who reproduces does not die

كل شمس إلها مغرب

Kul shams ilhā maghrib.

Every sun has its sunset

All good things come to an end

اللي عينه فارغة ما بيشبع

Illi 'aynu fārgha mā biyishba'.

He whose eye is greedy will never have a full stomach

Some people are never satisfied

قليل البخت يلاقى فى الكرشة عظمة

Galīl al bakht yilāgi fil karsha 'aẓma.

The unlucky man finds a bone in his tripe

cf. *The bread never falls but on its buttered side*

مش كل مرة بتسلم الجرة

Mish kul marra bitislam al jarra.

It is not every time that the clay pot survives

You cannot *tempt providence* and always triumph.

شحاذ وبيشارط

Shaḥādh wa biyshāriṭ.

A beggar and he bargains!

An example of audacity: cf. *Beggars can't be choosers*

اللي إيده بالمية ماهو زيّ اللي إيده بالنار

Illi idū fil mayya māhu zay illi idū fin-nār.

He who has his hand in the water is not like him who has his hand in the fire

Attitudes are formed by circumstances.

لا يلدغ المؤمن من جحر مرتين

Lā yuldagh al mu'min min juḥrin marratayn.

A wise man will not be bitten from a hole twice

Once bitten, twice shy

يتمسكن حتى يتمكن

Yitmaskan ḥatta yitmakkan.

He pretends to be humble until he has his chance

Once he is no longer dependent, he *changes his tune.*

إيش راح تعمل الماشطة بهذا الوجه الوحش

Aysh rāḥ ti 'mal al māshṭah bi hādha al wajh al wiḥish.

What can the lady comber do with this ugly face?

You cannot make a silk purse out of a sow's ear

أنا أمير وأنت أمير ومين حيسوق الحمير

Ana amīr wa inta amīr wa mīn ḥaysūg al ḥamīr.

I am a prince and you are a prince,
so who will drive the donkeys?

All Chiefs and no Indians

المال الحرام لا يدوم

Al māl al ḥarām lā yadūm.

Unlawful money does not last

Ill-gotten gains seldom prosper

القرد في عين أمه غزال

Al gird fi 'ayn ummu ghazāl.

In the eye of his mother a monkey is a gazelle

All her geese are swans

كل ما يعجبك والبس ما يعجب الناس

Kul mā yi 'jibak wa ilbis mā yi 'jib in-nās.

Eat what pleases you and wear what pleases others

cf. *Say as men say, but think to yourself*

ما بتنتصب الخيمة بوتد واحد

Mā bitintiṣib al khayma bi watad wāḥid.

A tent cannot be put up with one peg

روح بلّط البحر

Rūḥ balliṭ al baḥar.

Go tile the sea!

Get lost!

أكل الطعم وسرق الصنارة

Akal al tu'um wa sarag aṣ-ṣunnāra.

The fish ate the bait and stole the hook

cf. *to add insult to injury*

الصياد بيتقلى والعصفور بيتفلى

Iṣṣayād biyitgalla wal'aṣfūr biyitfalla.

The hunter seethes and the bird preens

One is unaffected by the desperation of the other.

الحسود لا يسود

Al ḥasūd lā yasūd.

The envious will not prevail

cf. *Envy eats nothing but its own heart*

لا ناقة لي فيها ولا جمل

La nāgata lī fīha walā jamal.

I have neither a male nor a female camel in it

cf. *it's no skin off my nose*

إذا قلت الخيول سرجوا الكلاب

Idha gallat al khuyūl sarrajū al kilāb.

From lack of horses they saddle dogs

There's nothing suitable, so they come up with a totally useless alternative.

إذا التقت العينان استحى اللسان

Idha iltagat al 'aynān istaḥa al lisān.

When eyes meet, the tongue becomes shy

It's easier to talk behind someone's back than to their face.

من أراد إغراق كلبه اتهمه بالجرب

Man arāda ighrāga kalbihi ittahamahu bil-jarab.

He who wants to drown his dog accuses him of mange

Give a dog a bad name and hang him

الديك الفصيح من البيضة يصيح

Ad dīk al faṣīḥ min al bayḍa yaṣīh.

The eloquent cock crows from the egg

cf. *It early pricks that will be a thorn*

الصبر مفتاح الفرج

Aṣ ṣabru muftāḥ al faraj.

Patience is the key to relief

ضربني وبكى وسبقني واشتكى

Ḍarabnī wa bakā wa sabagni washtakā.

He hit me and cried; he raced me to complain

It's all his fault, yet he pretends to be the victim!

على قد لحافك مد رجليك

'Alā gad liḥāfak mid rijlayk.

Stretch your legs according to the length of your quilt

Cut your coat according to your cloth

قرعة بتتباها بشعر بنت اختها

Gar'a bititbāhā bish'ar bint ukhtahā.

A bald woman brags about her niece's hair

مفتاح الشر كلمة

Muftāḩ al shar kilma.

The key to evil is one word

cf. *Of a small spark, a great fire*

لو بدها تشتي لغيمت

Law bidha tishti laghayyamat.

If it was going to rain it would have clouded over

إربط الحمار محل مايقول لك صاحبه

Urbuṭ al ḥimār maḥal mā yigūl lak ṣaḥibu.

Tie the donkey where his master tells you

An ass must be tied where his master will have him

إذا كان الكلام من فضة فالسكوت من ذهب

Idha kān al kalāmu min fiḍḍah fassukūtu min dhahab.

If speech is silver, silence is golden

A proverb shared by both languages.

من زرع الريح حصد العاصفة

Man zara'a ar rīḥ ḥaṣaḍa al'āṣifa.

He who sows the wind harvests the storm

Sow the wind and reap the whirlwind

الحمار حمار ولو بين الخيول رُبي

Al ḥimāru ḥimārun wa law bayn al khuyūli rubiya.

A donkey is a donkey even if he is raised among horses

If an ass goes a-travelling, he'll not come home a horse

من شب على شيء شاب عليه

Man shabba 'alā shay'in shāba 'alaihi.

He who grows with a habit greys with it

Old habits die hard

إتق شر من أحسنت إليه

Ittagi sharra man aḥsanta ilayhi.

Beware the evil of the man who has received your charity

cf. *to bite the hand that feeds you*

بطيختين بيد واحدة ما بيتحملوا

Baṭṭikhatayn bi yad wāḥida ma biyitḥamlu.

Two water melons cannot be carried in one hand

Don’t attempt the impossible.

كل تأخيرة فيها خيرة

Kul ta'khīra fīha khīra.

Every delay has its blessings

cf. *Every cloud has a silver lining*

إجى يكحلها عماها

Ijā yikāḥḥilha amāhā.

He came to apply kohl to the eye, he blinded it

cf. *to kill with kindness*

عصفور باليد خيرٌ من عشرة على الشجرة

'Aṣfūr bi al yad khayrun min 'ashra 'alā ash shajara.

Rather a bird in the hand than ten on the tree

A bird in the hand is worth two in the bush

نقول ثور يقول احلبوه

Nigūl thawr yigūl iḥlibū.

We say 'It's a bull', he says 'Milk it'

Don't confuse me with facts!

بيعطي الحلق للي بلا أودان

Biya'ṭi al ḥalag lilli bila awdān.

He gives earrings to the one without ears

. . . as pointless as *carrying coals to Newcastle*

ماكل مايتمنى المرء يدركه تجري الرياح بما لا تشتهي السفن

Mā kullu mā yatamanna al mar'u yudrikuhu tajri ar riyāḥu bimā la tashtahi as sufunu.

Man does not attain everything he desires;
Winds do not always blow as the vessels wish

Man proposes, God disposes

مقدمــة

«أعرف القوم من أمثالهم». قول عربي قديم.

ان هذا الكتاب الصغير الذي يحتوي على امثال عربية مترجمة الى اللغة الانكليزية يحاول فتح الباب لتعريف اهل الغرب على العرب وفيه يرى القاريء ان الكثير، بل الاكثرية من تلك الامثال لها ما يشابهها اما في النص او في المعنى من امثال الغرب.

وهذا يدحض الادعاء المأثور بأن «الشرق شرق والغرب غرب ولا يمكن التقاؤهما ابدا».

ورجاؤنا ان يساهم هذا الكتاب في التقاء الشرق والغرب لأن في ذلك الخلاص الحقيقي للبشر....

حاتم الخالدي، جدة

سنوات في البلاد العربية، وهي حاليا رسامة كاريكاتورية مؤسسة في انجلترا.

ونتهز هذه الفرصة لنشكر جميع من قدموا مساعدتهم لنا في اعداد هذا الكتاب وخاصة السيد حاتم الخالدي الذي منحنا وقته وارشاده وتشجيعه وتفضل علينا بكتابة المقدمة.

بريمروز ارناندر　　　　　　　　　　　　　اشخين سكيبويث

مقدمــة المؤلفــين

لقد جمعنا هذه الامثال والاقوال العربية آملين ان يتمتع بها القارئون العرب وغير العرب، واننا لا نعين انفسنا هنا كباحثين او عالمين في هذا الموضوع ولكننا نقدم الامثال والاقوال المستعملة يوميا التي جمعناها من الاصدقاء والزملاء. كما ان الامثلة ليست من بلد واحد او بلهجة معينة واحدة، ولكنها معروفة عامة في شرق العالم العربي.

تحت كل مثل عربي، نطبع ترجمة دقيقة بقدر الامكان، لمساعدة القراء الذين لا يعرفون اللغة. ونزود ايضا ترجمة انكليزية مطابقة بصدق للغة العربية، وفي اغلب الاحيان مع مثلٍ انجيلزي مشابه (بالحروف المائلة) او مع مقارنة مفيدة. وفي حالة عدم وجود مثل مشابه نعطي شرحاً قصيراً للمثل في المناسبات الخاصة.

ونعتبر انفسنا محظوظين جدا لاشتراك الرسامة كاثرين لام معنا فنيا، وخاصة انها قد امضت عدة

إبن البط عوام
نشرته مؤسسة ستايسي الدولية
١٢٨ كنسنجتون تشيرتش ستريت
لندن دبليو ٨ ٤ بي اتش
تلكس ٢٩٨٧٦٨ ستايسي جي

صف الحروف الانجليزية: شركة إس اكس كومبوزينج ليمتد،
اسكس، انجلترا على المونوفوتو، حرف بلانتن

صف الحروف العربية: اورورا برس ليمتد، لندن
حرف نسخي

طباعة وتجليد
بتلر آند تانر ليمتد، سومرست، انجلترا

إبـــن البـــط عـــوام

بريمروز أرناندر
اشخين سكيبويث

الرسوم التوضيحية
كاثرين لام

مؤسســة ستايســي الدوليــة
لنــدن